Sydny

D1406583

The ABC's of Physics
© 2014, Chris Ferrie

Atom

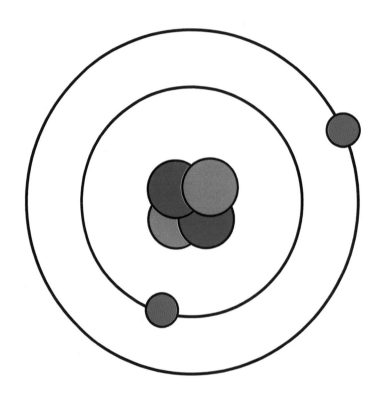

All things are made of atoms. Atoms are made of protons, electrons and neutrons. Atoms can combine to make molecules. When atoms smash together, they create a nuclear reaction.

Black hole

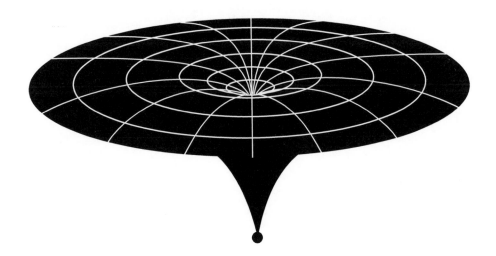

A black hole is a star so dense that not even light can escape its gravity. The boundary where this happens is called the event horizon. Many physicists believe that a very big black hole exists at the center of our galaxy.

Charge

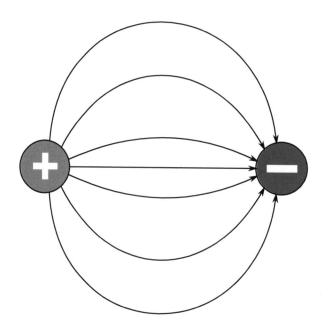

Charge is the physical property of matter which causes the effect of electrostatic attraction and repulsion. Charge can be positive or negative. Opposite charges are attracted and like charges are repelled.

Diffraction

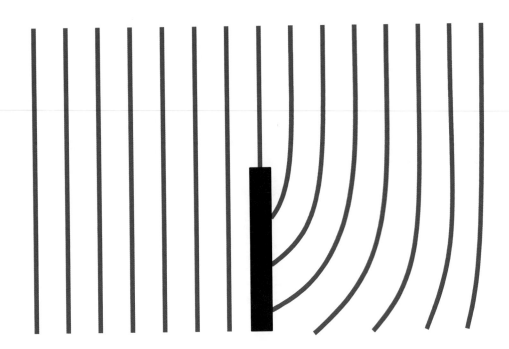

Diffraction occurs when a wave (water, light, sound, etc.) hits an object. When more than one object is hit, multiple diffraction events can create beautiful interference patterns.

Einstein

Albert Einstein is considered by many to be the greatest scientist to have lived. He made pioneering contributions to statistical physics and quantum theory. He also invented the theory of relativity.

Fusion

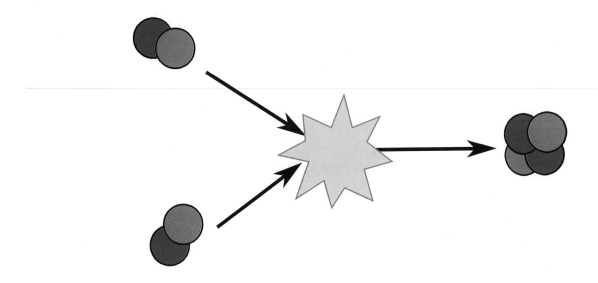

Fusion happens when two atoms collide and create a new atom. For some atoms, a lot of energy is created by this process. The sun is constantly fusing hydrogen into helium.

Gravity

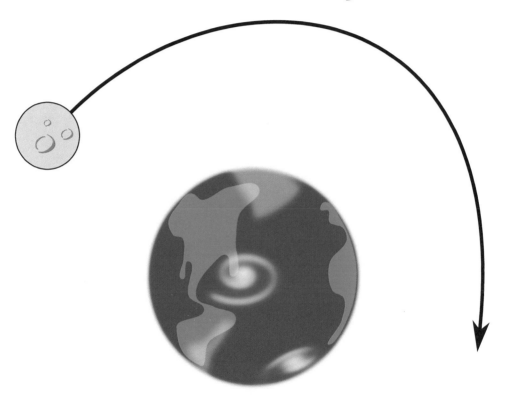

Gravity is the force that causes things to be attracted to each other, like the earth and moon. Gravity keeps the moon in orbit around earth and also brings us back down when we jump.

Heat

Heat is the transfer of energy from something hot to something cold. Fire is hot and gives off heat to its cooler surroundings. The sun is very hot and gives heat to the earth.

Ion

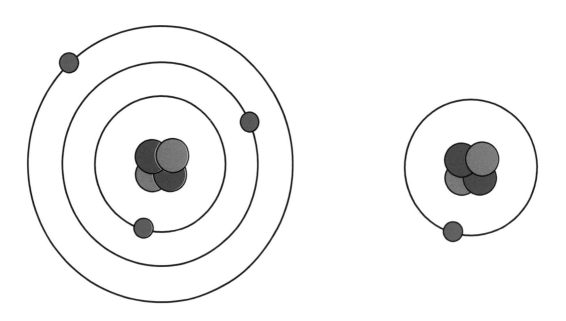

An ion is an atom that has more or less electrons than it has protons. An ion with more electrons has negative charge and an ion with less electrons has postive charge. Making an ion is called ionization.

Joule

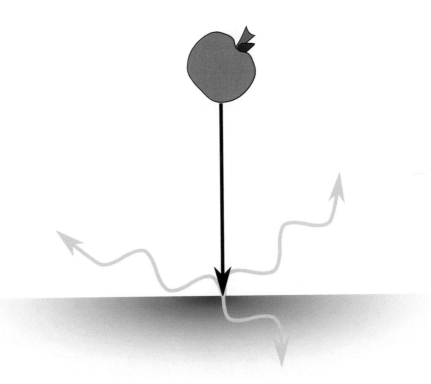

A Joule is the standard unit of energy. One Joule is the
amount of energy released when a large apple falls one
foot to the ground. The Joule is named after physcist
James Joule who worked on thermodynamics.

Kelvin

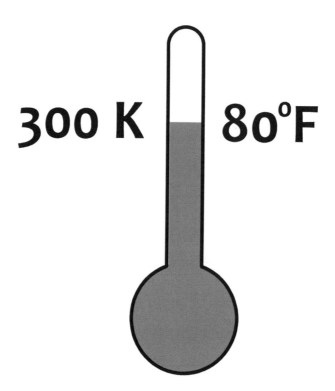

300 K | 80°F

A Kelvin is the standard unit of temperature. The temperature where you are reading this book is close to 300 Kelvin. It was named after physicist William Thomson who later became Lord Kelvin.

Liquid

Liquid, solid and gas are the three primary states of matter. If a liquid gets too hot, it turns to gas. If it gets too cold, it turns to solid. Water is the liquid form of the compound H_2O. Boiling water turns it to gas—freezing it, to ice.

Magnet

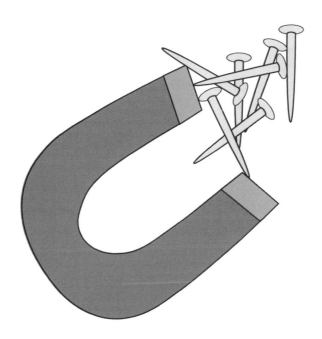

Magnets create magnetic fields which interact with all matter. Other magnets are affected the most. Magnets arise from either inate atomic properties or electric currents.

Newton

A Newton is the standard unit of force. It is named after physicist Isaac Newton. Newton is famous for his laws of motion which govern the dynamics of matter under the influence of forces. He also invented calculus.

Optics

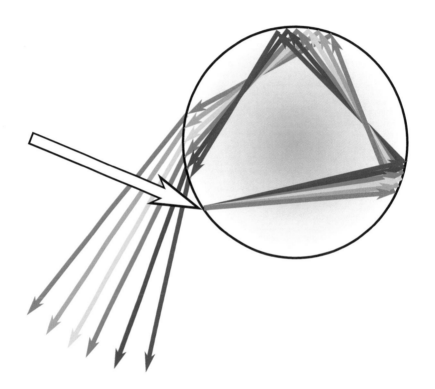

Optics is the study of how light interacts with matter. It helped with the invention of eyeglasses and telescopes. After the quantum nature of light was discovered, the study of optics lead to lasers.

Photon

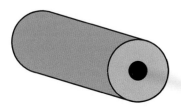

A photon is the elementary particle which carries the electromagnetic force, which includes light, lasers, radio and x-rays. Photons have no mass and no electric charge. Humans can see as little as 5 photons.

Quantum

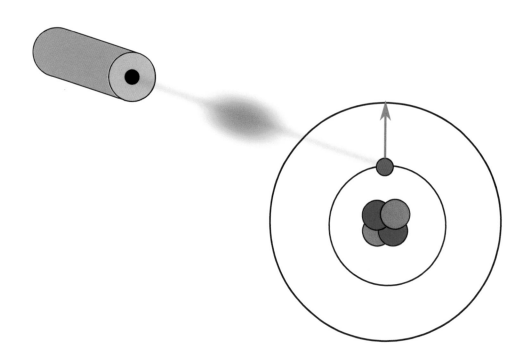

Quantum theory best describes the interactions of energy and matter at microscopic scales, like atoms and photons. Through quantum engineering, we are trying to allow these effects to occur at macroscopic (large) scales.

Relativity

Einstein's theory of relativity states that the effect of gravity is due to a warping of spacetime. The theory has predicted many extraordinary things such as black holes, gravity waves and wormholes.

String theory

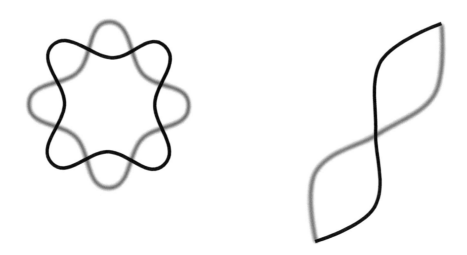

String theory is a candidate "theory of everything" which combines quantum theory with relativity. It replaces the idea of particles (protons, electrons, etc.) with vibrating strings.

Thermodynamics

Work!

Thermodynamics is the study of how heat and temperature are related to energy and how we can use energy to do work for us. A famous law of thermodynamics says that heat cannot flow from something cold to something hot.

Uncertainty

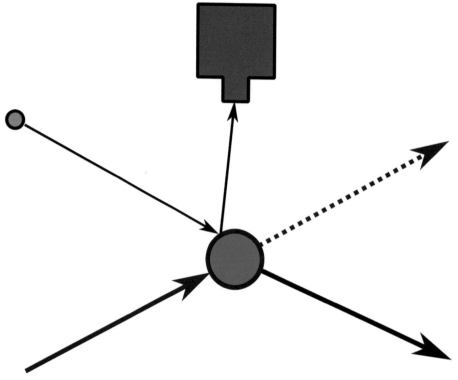

Heinsenberg's uncertainty principle states that when one property of a system is measured, another property is disturbed. So, we can not know both where a particle is and where it is going.

Vacuum

Vacuum is a space that has nothing in it. Even outer space has some particles floating around. The idea of vacuum is useful for thinking about what would happen in ideal conditions to carry out experiments.

Wavelength

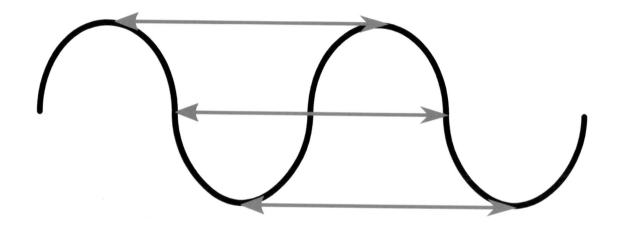

Repeating patterns like ripples in water or vibrations on a string are called waves. The distance over which the pattern repeats is called the wavelength. We can hear sound waves in air with wavelengths as little as 1 inch.

X-ray

X-ray radiation is high energy light which we can not see. X-rays have a very short wavelength and can go through our skin but not our bones. This makes them useful for medicine and security.

Yttrium

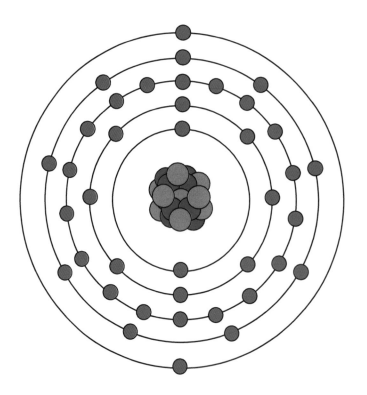

Yttrium is one of the many elements. There is one element
for every number of protons in the nucleus. Yttrium has
39 protons and so is recognized in the periodic table by the
number 39 or the symbol "Y".

Zero-point

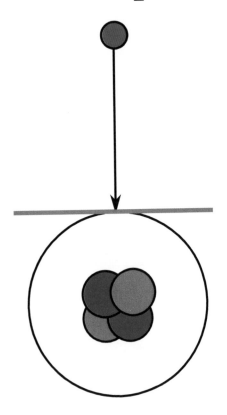

Before quantum theory, it was thought that things could have zero energy. But quantum theory predicts that the lowest possible energy of any thing is not zero. This amount of energy is called the zero-point energy.

Chris Ferrie is a physicist, mathematician and father of three budding young scientists. He obtained his doctorate in Mathematical Physics from the University of Waterloo in Waterloo, Canada and currently holds a postdoctoral fellowship at the University of New Mexico in Albuquerque, New Mexico.

Chris believes it is never too early to introduce children to the wild and wonderful world of physics!

Congrats!
I hope you enjoy ur
time off! Good LUCK!
    - SERAFINA

have fun with your new child!

    ᵔ JACK WELCH

Congrats!
Have lots of fun with
your baby!

    - Keenan Gamache

Congrats!
Good luck, and hope
you have a good next couple
months with your new baby!
    - Sophie Blanchard

Good luck!
    -Natalie
    Panteleos

Tell the baby
I say "Hi"

    - Spencer Pickett

Made in the USA
Lexington, KY
08 January 2015